SCISSORSCRAFT

**LITTLE
CRAFT BOOK
SERIES**

written and illustrated
by LINI GROL

 STERLING PUBLISHING CO., INC.   NEW YORK
SAUNDERS OF TORONTO, Ltd.,   Don Mills, Canada

 Oak Tree Press Co., Ltd.
London & Sydney

Little Craft Book Series

Beads Plus Macramé
Big-Knot Macramé
Candle-Making
Coloring Papers
Corrugated Carton Crafting
Creating with Beads
Creating with Burlap
Creating with Flexible Foam
Enamel without Heat
Felt Crafting
Flower Pressing
Macramé
Making Paper Flowers

Masks
Metal and Wire Sculpture
Model Boat Building
Nail Sculpture
Needlepoint Simplified
Off-Loom Weaving
Potato Printing
Puppet-Making
Repoussage
Scissorscraft
Sewing without a Pattern
Tole Painting
Whittling and Wood Carving

For Karen, Carl and Alex

Third Printing, 1972
Copyright © 1970 by Sterling Publishing Co., Inc.
419 Park Avenue South, New York, N.Y. 10016
Simultaneously Published and Copyright © 1970 in Canada
by Saunders of Toronto, Ltd., Don Mills, Ontario
British edition published by Oak Tree Press Co., Ltd., Nassau, Bahamas
Distributed in Australia by Oak Tree Press Co., Ltd.,
P.O. Box 34, Brickfield Hill, Sydney 2000, N.S.W.
Distributed in the United Kingdom and elsewhere in the British Commonwealth
by Ward Lock Ltd., 116 Baker Street, London W 1
Manufactured in the United States of America   *All rights reserved*
Library of Congress Catalog Card No.: 70–126849
ISBN 0–8069– 5160–5   UK 7061 2264 X
5161–3

Contents

Before You Begin 4

Scissors Cuttings 6

    Bunny 6

    Leaf 10

    Flowers 14

    Mirrored Pictures 19

Human Figures 20

Compositions of Several Figures 24

Valentines 31

Balance In Your Designs 33

Mounting Cuttings on a Background 34

Making Prints from Scissors Cuttings 36

Some Printed Pictures 39

Index 48

Before You Begin

Remember when you were young and cut valentines from paper for your sweetheart? You were using one of the oldest art forms known, the art of scissors cutting! Dating back to 300 B.C., scissors cutting has been a royal pastime in European and Asian courts throughout history. Because this hobby is so much fun, even children love to create with it. When carefully and artistically done, many scissors cuttings are hung in museums all over the world.

Can you cut paper well enough to merit a place in a museum? Chances are that your work will be good enough to hang in your own home, at least, where your friends will see the lovely compositions, and maybe ask for samples of your work for themselves. Design your own original greeting cards, and they will be remembered and commented on for years to come. Make prints from your original paper cutting. Put silhouettes between clear plastic for dramatic placemats or book covers, or under glass on a table top to add a new touch to your home.

Do not get discouraged if you make a few mistakes at first—if your scissors slip or the cuts you make are not quite as fine as you might wish. Just remember that practice makes perfect, and you are bound to improve if you keep at it. Your mistakes may make lovely designs themselves.

To find out if you are a great scissorscraft artist, you need to gather only a few simple materials from their various places around your home:

PAPER: Experiment to find what types and thicknesses are most suitable for you and your project. Different scenes and varying amounts of detail call for different weights of paper. For example, a row of tiny ballerinas would be cut most easily from tissue paper, while a big house, involving long straight cuts and square corners, should be made from heavy construction paper.

SCISSORS: Have several sizes on hand to use on different parts of your cutting. Use a large pair for making the outline, and smaller ones to cut into your design. Fine scissors will work best when you have to make very little cuts—to detail a face, for example, or for thin lines in a leaf or flower.

In addition to the length of the blades, there is another important difference among scissors: the sharpness of the points. Some blades have rounded tips, but these are not a wise choice for scissorscraft, as there is a limited amount of detail you can make with this kind of scissors. To cut details in your designs, the most practical is therefore a pair with extremely pointed tips. You will be able to make very small snips with your scissors, at the same time being able to see where you are cutting. Your chances of making a mistake are much less using pointed scissors for detail than using those with rounded blades.

CARDBOARD: You will want heavy cardboard to use as backing material for your delicate designs. The durability of the cardboard will ensure that your work will not be crushed or folded. Use cardboard of a shade that contrasts with the paper to achieve a more spectacular picture.

GLUE: To attach the cutting on to its cardboard backing, a mucilage is best. Use the glue sparingly, as a little goes a long way. If you use too much glue, it will ooze over the edges of your picture and spoil the clean lines that are a part of this art.

SPACE: Lots of space is necessary, for glue unfortunately tends to go into the wrong places. Perhaps you can even set aside a corner of your home to make your exclusive workspace.

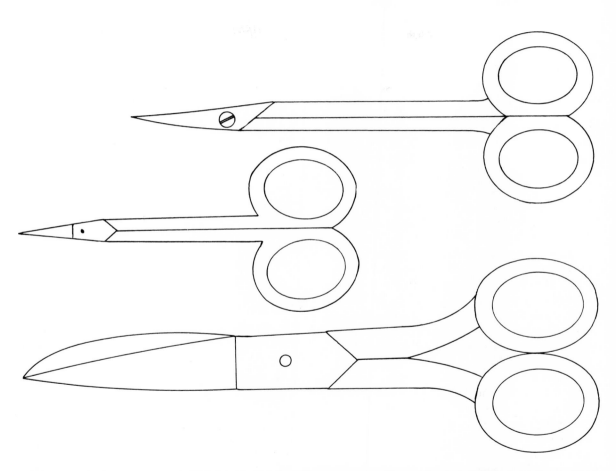

Have at least three kinds of scissors on hand while you are cutting. The top pair is best for cutting detailed outlines, the middle and finest pair makes the smallest snips inside a design, and the bottom pair can quickly and accurately cut large areas.

Scissors Cuttings

Bunny

The adorable bunny in Illus. 1 could decorate an Easter basket, or, made larger, be framed to hang in a child's room. Using your big pair of scissors, cut 4 or 5 rabbits at the same time from several layers of paper. To ensure that your bunny looks like what he is supposed to, sketch his outline on

Illus. 1. This bunny rabbit is very cute the way he appears here, but you can add details to make him even more appealing.

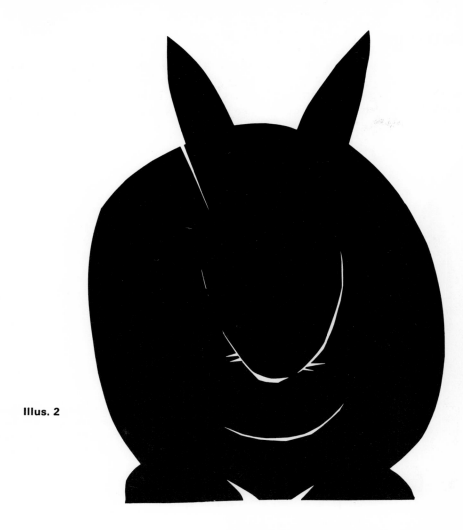

Illus. 2

to the top paper before you cut. It is easy to correct a pencil sketch, but nearly impossible to repair a figure that was cut incorrectly.

Now use smaller scissors to add detail to the bunny's body. One way to get inside the figure with your scissors is to make a cut from the edge straight into the body. Don't worry about the cut showing. If you only go over the cut once, and if

you glue the two sides together when mounting on cardboard, the cut will not show at all. In Illus. 2, the cut alongside the bunny's ear was made a bit thicker than it should have been to show you just how to get into the body. Once you have made this cut, shape the head, neck and paws with your fine scissors.

Cut into the body again, this time for the inner ears. And cut into his face to make his eyes and nose, as in Illus. 3.

Illus. 4

In Illus. 4, even his fur has been detailed on one side of his body. Naturally, you would use very fine scissors to make these tiny cuts. From the inner ear, make the lines between his eyes to give a cute expression to your bunny's face. Is he worried? Or has he spied some food? When you have added details to your satisfaction, glue this happy hopper on to stiff cardboard to keep him still, and hang him in a prominent place. Then, get ready for compliments!

9

Leaf

You say that you cannot even cut a straight line? Don't despair! Few things in nature occur with exact symmetry or straightness. Study a leaf, for example. Notice how one side is different from the other, and that no two leaves are exactly alike —Mother Nature creates diversity! Cut a leaf the way you want, and no one will be able to claim that it is not a copy of a real leaf. You can cut a leaf freehand (that is, without drawing it first) or you may trace the outline of a real leaf on to the paper. Don't forget to make the stem—and because you are the artist, you can make it as long as you want.

Illus. 5. A leaf can be any size or shape you want it to be, or any size and shape that you happen to cut.

Illus. 6

Once you have cut the outline of your leaf, you will want to distinguish it by showing what kind of a leaf it is. Again, your best inspiration is to study a real leaf. Notice the edges—do they have points, or are they smooth? And if there are dents, do they run in an upward or a downward direction? There is a great deal of difference between the delicate points of the weeping willow leaf and the bold curves of an oak.

Now turn the leaf over and examine the veins on its underside. In Illus. 7, some veins have been cut out, using small scissors. Notice that every vein that appears on a real leaf is not cut out here! Such a job would take infinite patience and would actually detract from the effect that only a few cuts suggest. To get inside the leaf, cut straight in from the edge, going over the cut only once with the scissors to make a clean slash. The cut to the inside will not show later.

If you want to make your leaf more elaborate and show more of the background, as in Illus. 8, try "hollow cutting," or cutting out a section on the inside of the leaf without making a cut from the edge. To do this, use your fine pointed scissors and make a little hole with a pin right in the middle of the area you want to cut out. You will be able to insert a point of the scissors into the rip and cut out the proper area.

Illus. 8

Flowers

The outline of a simple flower appears in Illus. 9. Use your large scissors if you copy this design to make a long, curving shape. Illus. 10 shows the same flower after it has been hollow cut, with no slit from the outside edge into the petals. Until you become expert at this technique of cutting the flower with your scissors, proceed cautiously. Don't cut too close to the edge of the flower, or you might tear the paper or cut through to the edge. It is better to cut away too little than too much, as you can always trim later if you decide to.

Illus. 10

Illus. 9

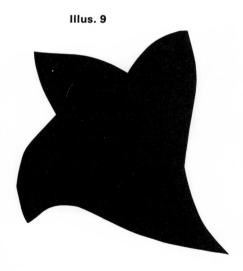

14

Illus. 11

Illus. 12

For a change, put the middle of the flower in a different place, to show the flower from varying angles. (See Illus. 11 and 12.)

If you want your flower to be identical on both sides, the easiest method is to fold the paper in half and cut only one side of the flower. Then when you open the paper up, the fold line will be down the middle of the flower, and since they were cut together, both sides will be the same. See Illus. 13 for an example of a folded flower. After opening, the right side was slightly modified to improve its appearance. If you want to make two sides similar but not identical, cut them by folding, and then add different details to each side.

Now that you have made both flowers and leaves, try a floral design combining both of these natural beauties. Use a few layers of paper to cut out several patterns at once, and then, using your fine pointed scissors, hollow cut each of them

Illus. 13. Folding a piece of paper in half and then cutting it will make a design which is symmetrical along the fold line.

Illus. 14

separately so that they do not resemble each other at all. The flowers in Illus. 14 and 15 were cut out together, for example, but in Illus. 14 only the veins were made. The hollow cuts on the flower in Illus. 15 make the arrangement lighter and more delicate, and the pattern can be seen from a dis-

tance. Make a large floral composition to hang on the wall in a sunny room—add several flowers cut from different colored papers, and some green leaves, and place them all on a blue background. This is one flower arrangement that will never die, and you do not even have to water it!

Mirrored Pictures

The swans in Illus. 16 seem to be realistically reflected in a pool of water. Actually, this picture was made by cutting the swans in quadruplicate (that is, four figures at once). To do this, fold a piece of paper into quarters, so that there are four thicknesses. Then draw and cut the figure you want to have, being careful not to cut through the folds where the figures will remain attached. The "real life" swans here were detailed by hollow cutting, while their reflections lack features and are glassy, as the surface of a pool would actually reflect.

Another use for mirrored pictures is to separate the top and bottom rows, and then attach the two strings side by side to form one continuous line. You could then use the row as a repeating motif on a lamp shade, or on anything that you want to decorate in this way.

Illus. 16

Human Figures

Now that you have experimented with cutting out flowers and other natural scenes, try your hand at human figures. Remember the paper dolls you cut out when you were in grade school? The little man in Illus. 17 is closely related. Cut several figures and dress each one differently for an entire paper family.

Illus. 17

Illus. 18

Perhaps you would like to dress one figure up with a fancy collar and cuffs. Hollow cutting is the best way to cut out such a large area. Begin by making just a small hole with a sharp pin in the middle of his chest; it will then be easier to add details if you have already cut away most of the excess.

You can add details by cutting in from the outside edge, if you find this technique easier. Now this little man has pants, and buttons on his shirt.

The slash on his face was made wide purposely to show you how his facial features were cut from the edge rather than by hollow cutting.

Illus. 19

Illus. 20

Even though the fancy dresser in Illus. 20 is facing in another direction and has very different features than the other three figures here, he was cut at the same time as the others. Fine scissors were used to add much detail here. The stripes in his pants, his jacket, sleeves and cuffs, and even his face were hollow cut. When making a picture with so much detail, it pays to plan your design before you cut. Light pencil marks can guide you and prevent the disastrous mistakes that come from cutting too freely.

Compositions of
Several Figures

An arrangement of two objects—animals, leaves, human figures—calls for careful planning, for the positions and proportions of each part will make the entire picture a pleasing one, or one that misses by making the viewer feel he must tilt his head to look at the picture. In Illus. 21 and 22, there are two steps shown in making an arrangement of two frogs and some cattails, all cut from

Illus. 21

Illus. 22

the same piece of paper. Before you even pick up your scissors, lightly sketch where you plan to cut. If the design does not appeal to you now, it cer-

tainly will not later, either, so plan ahead, and do not be afraid to change your mind or try different combinations.

Illus. 23

The pair of Dutch dolls holding hands (Illus. 23) is made by prefolding. To make the folds and ruffles on the apron of the doll on the right, fine scissors were used to cut from the outside in. The left doll could remain solid, to represent the right one's shadow, or she could be cut so that she is wearing different clothes. A doll and her shadow? Twin sisters? Or just two girls standing together? How you cut their clothes will tell their story.

The piper in Illus. 24 and 25 is more difficult than anything you have tried yet, but if you do a good job, you will be proud of your struggle. This little man would make a nice greeting card to announce the birth of a boy. In Illus. 24, only the silhouette has been made, mostly by hollow cutting. Notice how the high tree on the right side balances the leaves on the left, while both act as a natural frame for the piper himself. Consider these things when you plan.

Illus. 24

In Illus. 25, the piper is dressed up a bit. His hat now has a fancy ribbon, and the tiny slit for his eye gives his face a whimsical expression which would be ruined by adding more details. There are many items in this picture—why ruin it by hollow cutting everything? In this case, just a little work goes a long way.

Illus. 25

Illus. 26

The mothers in Illus. 26 and 27 show again how different you can make two identical patterns. While these ladies were cut at the same time, one was turned over so she would face in the other

direction. Then, details were added—in one, emphasis is on the baby's body, while in the other, the mother's expression is what you notice first.

Try a few of this type of design yourself. It could make a wonderful Christmas card, or a congratulatory card for a new mother.

Valentines

Remember when you cut your first valentine? Your new hobby should give you inspiration to create much more elaborate hearts than you used to cut. Cut the middle figures large, so you can shape them as you like. As you can probably tell, the heart in Illus. 28 is a folded cut, so that each side of the heart is symmetrical.

Illus 28. Next Valentine's Day, elaborate on your basic heart outline by adding faces and border designs to show how much you care.

And here are the lovers! In spite of the many cuts and the apparent detail here, the design in Illus. 29 is really very simple. Triangles were cut and ruffles made along the outside. Keep the heart folded while you cut border decorations, as you will then be able to do both sides at once, making them identical. For your first try, cut a valentine from a large piece of paper to provide space for your scissors to work in. If you wish, lighten the faces by hollow cutting, as you did with the human figure in Illus. 20. If you have enough paper, cut some flowers and arrange them around your valentine. Hearts and flowers are always a welcome gift!

Balance in Your Designs

Now that you have practiced for a while, you can probably cut with some ability. But there is more to the art of scissorscraft than just cutting. Remember that proportion, position and design are important considerations, and that the type of scene you have in mind determines what kind of paper and scissors you should use.

Illus. 30. The branches and leaves make a natural frame for the girl in the picture. Even though this cutting has four square corners, the design is rounded and graceful.

Compare Illus. 30 and 31. Both were thought about but not drawn before the artist began cutting. If you are expert, you will be able to cut without a pencil design. At first, however, it is best to sketch the composition.

Both designs are naturally framed with the leaves and branches which form an important part of their design. Notice also that neither is hollow cut at all—why not? Because the scenes are delicate enough without adding more white space. In Illus. 30, specifically, the flowers and the young girl are slender and graceful, and almost seem to be in motion. If you try to copy this scene, use tissue paper and very fine scissors to achieve the thin stems and fragile petals shown here.

The scene in Illus. 31 has less detail: its lines are strong and straight. You could use construction paper for this silhouette, and a larger pair of scissors to make the long, sweeping curves. Practice cutting curves on a spare piece of paper before you begin your picture—it's easy!

Illus. 31. While the branches of the scene in Illus. 30 form a frame, the ones here make an archway for the girl and the deer.

Mounting Cuttings on a Background

Once you have cut a picture that you really like, you will want to preserve it. Since many cuttings are as delicate as cobwebs, the best way to ensure a lasting piece of art is to glue it on to stiff cardboard. A shade contrasting that of the cutting is often pretty. Glueing is an important step, so be very careful! You would not want to ruin a fragile scissors cutting by carelessly handling it at the last moment.

First, decide exactly where the cutting should be on its backing. Now put a blob of glue on a small piece of cardboard, and dip the end of a strip of paper about 2 by 2½ inches into the glue. Slide the glue-covered part of the strip very carefully under the cutting, while holding a major part of the art in place. If the cutting is big, glue the middle first and then fasten the four corners. Every inch of the cutting does not have to be glued, but make sure that you fasten the major areas so that the picture cannot rip or fold over on itself. To find out if there are any loose places, blow softly over the picture, and notice where any loose areas come up.

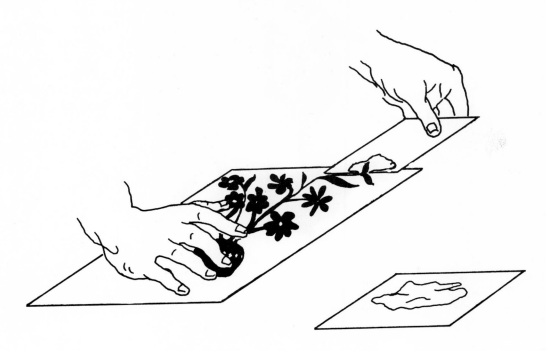

Making Prints from Scissors Cuttings

You can make prints from your cuttings, to use on greeting cards or stationery. Just think of sending Christmas cards with your own name in the design itself! Make your cutting from thick, soft, absorbent construction paper. While the cutting in Illus. 32 could be mounted and used as a decoration that way, it was made to be used as a pattern for painting. You could spray it with

Illus. 32. This cutting was made from very stiff cardboard, so that it would still be sturdy after being sprayed with paint.

Illus. 33

paint from an aerosol can, or spatter-paint it, using an old toothbrush. The paper in Illus. 33 was the background upon which the cutting rested while it was sprayed. If you want to use this background paper as your final picture, be very careful while spraying or spattering not to let the cutting move, as paint would get on to the areas you want to keep white.

Illus. 34. This is a print of the leaf in Illus. 32. After the original cutting was sprayed with paint, it was pressed on to another piece of paper, to make a duplicate design of the cutting.

Another way to use your cutting is to spray the cutting itself, and then turn it paint side down and press it on to another piece of paper. You will have printed (by pressing) the same design as the one you cut, only reversed, and now there is no danger of the picture falling off or being damaged.

For truly professional results, take your mounted cutting to a printer. He will photograph it and make a printing plate, either letterpress or offset.

Then he will put the plate on a small press where he will be able to control the inking so that all parts of the picture are uniformly dark. He can enlarge or reduce the size of your cutting when photographing it, and print any number of copies you wish. Why not design a Christmas card with a personal scene of your own? Have the printer make several hundred cards for you. Your friends will marvel at your creativity.

Some Printed Pictures

The designs in Illus. 35, 36 and 37 were printed on notepaper. Because the cuttings were so delicate, painting them or leaving them mounted would not have been wise.

Illus. 35

Illus. 36

The composition in Illus. 38 was used to announce a Hallowe'en party. The original could also have been hung at party time to enhance the eerie atmosphere.

Illus. 37

Illus. 38

The cuttings of Indians in Illus. 39, 40, 41 and 42 are so finely done that even the fringe on their clothing and the ragged edges of their feathers show. Use your finest scissors if you cut something this detailed.

Illus. 39

Illus. 40

Illus. 41

Illus. 42

Illus. 43

46

Nature pictures are fun to do, for you are free to add branches or bugs at will. The wings in Illus. 43 and 44 are hollow cut to show the transparent appearance of a butterfly.

Illus. 44. By using pointed scissors and taking the utmost care, you will soon be able to cut the most delicate scenes yourself. Any scene —natural or man-made—is suitable for scissorscraft.

Index

balance, 33–34
boy, 20–23
bunny, 6–9
butterflies, 46–47
cardboard, 4
complex compositions, 24–30
compositions of several figures, 24–30
design, 33–34
Dutch dolls, 26
floral compositions, 17–18
flowers, 14–18
folded cuttings, 16
frog, 24–25
glue, 4
glueing cutting on cardboard, 35
Hallowe'en cutting, 41
hearts, 31–32
history, 4
hollow cutting, 13
human figures, 20–23

Indians, 42–45
leaf, 10–13
materials, 4–5
mirrored pictures, 19
mother and child, 29–30
mounting on cardboard, 35
painting a cutting, 36–38
paper, types of, 4
piper, 27–28
planning a design, 23, 25, 33–34
prints, 36–38
proportion, 33–34
rabbit, 6–9
scissors, 4–5
spatter-painting, 36–38
spray painting, 36–38
stencil, using cutting as 36–38
swans, 19
uses for cuttings, 4
valentines, 31–32